UROOJ

IBRAHIM

This collection of poems is dedicated to nature- my tutor, baba, mama, my aunt and the people who came and left.

Preface

The poems in this book follow the rhythm of balance. Inspired by the equilibrium presented to us by life- from merry to gloomy days, perfectly balanced by life. From orderly formats to free, wild nature of poems, the rhythm has it all!

The poems have been written with a sense of pity on others and to myself, with the intention that it might be of some help to the readers, mostly the confused youth, who found themselves wedged by the notion of following the good or following the ways taken by, most of the classes. A try, to call the age group same as me to not follow or understand but to feel the poems, and learn to learn from nature.

The eyes of poor

(SONNET)

Partake whose mouth the pebbles in, amidst

us, throat of pity, don't feel the distress

of gulping trenchet edge of glass; whorl wrist

around glass, hurled by heathen, who suppress.

The grief of clouds, take hold of you, yourself;

For they are stressed by their own contretemps,

how can you lessen, weeping, when yourself

discerning clearly, raining the attempts.

With snug embosom of the breathing wealth,

enjoying the unjust bread in abode;

What do they get but dreich embrace of death,

the marching feet on jagged road, corrode.

    Yet your sleep is unhinged by lusty life;

    yet they enjoy a sleep that's full of life.

Let it rain-insane!

Sheltered by an umbrella, you say, you love rain;

poignant drops, burry some in their grave.

Some don't have hands to cover, some walk in pouring pain;

still you will sing the relief of rain, showing your dance to a slave.

Only if I could screen them with my eye lids, I would;

walk in a sand storm then, I would.

Don't worry the time will pass, dear admirer;

don't worry the time will pass, dear abhorrer.

Bread

The mellow doesn't flower my buds,

Maybe it was not raised by a confectioner.

The loaf doesn't nurture my innocent bloods,

Was it, maybe not made by the lightest barley, dear.

The lips don't stretch, not even a slender smile,

The reason surely should be, it wasn't much of a pile.

There aren't the emotions of tranquillity or joy,

Maybe because I tyrannically stole it from the boy.

Reasons

(Cinquain)

Reason;

the lone reason

that my tears didn't taste salt;

the very, made my hurdling heart halt.

Reason...

Comma

(SONNET)

What merry whisper, will your ears, shall hear,

when chirp of summer sparrow, will turn in

the voidness, felt in bones, at dusk of year;

this is the order of life, not your sin.

When lustrous leaf of the one we adore,

no longer cover the sun's blazing heat.

We will be walking, under the cloud, sore,

Hard bread in mouth and no bouquet to eat.

Your own name, is not waiting to be called;

the wing of butterfly knows, it won't last;

the rain knows ,it forever, won't applaud;

the crows know the peace will come though, at last.

    Some folks are comma to our book of life,

    while some are just a comma to our life.

Drown

(Cinquain)

The gown

of youth fell down;

to find pair of warm hands,

only to grab the void of limp sand.

All drown.

Dear mortal

(Cinquain)

Deceive,

my thoughts do deceive

me, walking with mortal

forms a dream, stays immortal,

still leaves.

The bud we all grew

(SONNET)

When the reflection stares in your pride soul;

don't poison, pious pond with sullied lake.

For it, the beauty not lie In blue – foul,

the beauty lie in virtue, like snow flake.

Why to halt, loving the dove, crow alike?

Why did you stop believing in fond heart?

what did they do to you my dear, the like

you said, won't be you, now beats in your heart.

The closest thing to god our childish hearts

were, the next thing to dew our pure tears were;

look at us now dear, heavy heathen hearts

world full of wealth yet not the heart to share

    We all are killers of our inner child

    All cowards, yet have the good guts to hide.

Still they compare!

In this sparkling dark ocean of life,

never a shore was struck by the same wave;

never a poet, saw the poem with same life;

a swift stroke and the soil, back to grave.

Nauseating noise, nudging us to the lead,

led by the crawling lianas, for a seed.

So close your eyes and walk the path;

So walk walk and walk, without the worry of the wrath.

Give them back!

(Cinquain)

15

The sigh.

Justice, is it

Or trial, who knows, won't try.

Give me my tears, I want to cry,

amidst.

What am I?

(Cinquain)

16

My wish?

Am I too much,

knowing or a foolish.

All I say, oppose the world's wish,

as such.

Photos

(Cinquain)

17

I see,

how the heart flea,

when eyes struck on photos,

giving that dusty looking pose.

Memory...

You are perfect!

Spent the fleshy fruits of our life,

In an idea that doesn't exist- perfect;

Something, that put between you and peace, a strife,

something that discern man and the maker of manly intellect.

So thank- for the pulp that fell for you,

for finding simple, which is best for you.

If only the man could realize, the worth of grain, he eat;

if only the peacock would admire his quill and not look at it's feet.

Before the time is over

(SONNET)

Your head-high, aiming at the building, high;

pride walk like lion, winning him a bride,

Yet your head low, when drops fall in July,

tall trees whined, soil and shovel when collide.

Warm nature grew small saplings with meek rain,

the present mother grows the little ones

in cunning mist and under the dull pain;

stop teaching the way of pride, to young ones.

Distinct are both my dear, pride and esteem;

one devil's tool, another the God's gift.

So lower your gaze, even in bright theme,

smile with a heart before the streel soil shift.

    The whole youth in becoming rare, you threw,

    still couldn't be barely better than you, you...

Grace!

(Cinquain)

His grace!

It's God's great grace;

without words, sang the birds,

his will, put life in poet's words.

His grace...

Finding a way

Let's pray with hearts one, like a mother and her foetus,

pray till the soul gets pious from corrupt,

till the stone heart melts, of ours;

pray till the death disrupt.

Prayed enough prayers,

where only thing taken was our tears;

a way of pray that turns to mothers touch, the knife,

a way of pray that takes our life.

Faith

(Cinquain)

Faith,

do we have Faith?

Or way of forerunners,

and we are mere their followers.

Faith?

Praise be to the one

(Cinquain)

23

Doubt me,

they all doubt me.

Can't complain, when myself

I don't praise the one, who himself

made me!

Fake skin

Look at them, smile slender like a crescent;

waiting, like a venal agent, with wide pupil,

for the grains to grow, of a peasant,

to take an unjust share without a scruple.

Hear it! All the applause,

having a cunning cause;

All these applause raining in the air,

only a few reaching the lips- despair...

More then that

(Cinquain)

25

A home,

build us a home;

don't just build us a house,

don't waste the trickling life, my spouse.

A home...

For you, oh! Dead one

Wish I could remember the first time-

on the 8th of December, my skin feeling the air,

must have been cold, surely wintertime,

when they saw me for first time, in pair.

The first word, first walk, must have been a feeling,

The joy in the pair of composer, must have blown the ceiling.

Wish I could feel all the firsts again, and remember,

the seventeen years till I was born on 22nd November.

www.ingramcontent.com/pod-product-compliance
Lightning Source LLC
Chambersburg PA
CBHW020657160726
47991CB00003B/1230